THE RICORDI
SONATINA ALBUM

FOR PIANO

Lower Intermediate to Intermediate Level

RICORDI

E.R. 3017

CONTENTS

LUDWIG VAN BEETHOVEN (1770-1827)

Sonatina in G Major

(Anh. 5, No. 1)

Moderato

1.

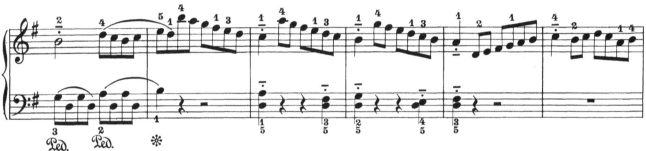

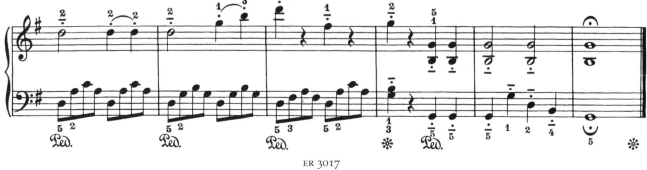

Romanza

z

5

MUZIO CLEMENTI (1752-1832)
Sonatina in C Major

(Op. 36, No. 1)

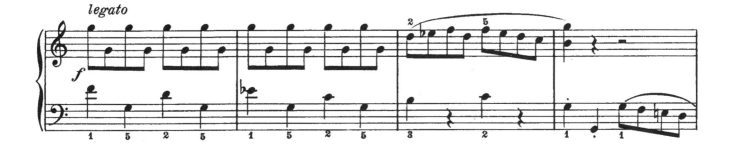

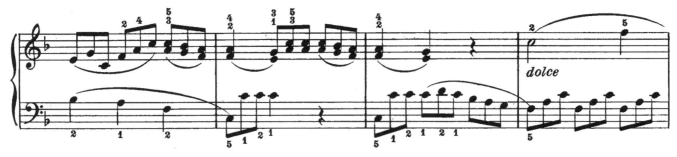

MUZIO CLEMENTI
Sonatina in C Major

(Op. 36, No. 3)

Un poco adagio

Allegro

MUZIO CLEMENTI
Sonatina in F Major

(Op. 36, No. 4)

4.

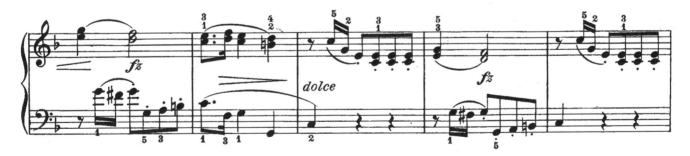

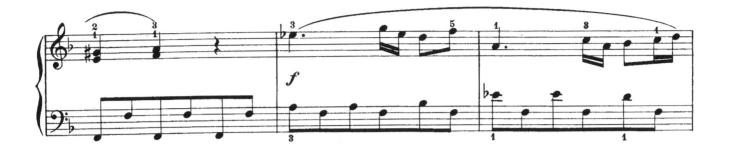

And.^{te} con espressione

RONDÒ

Allº vivace

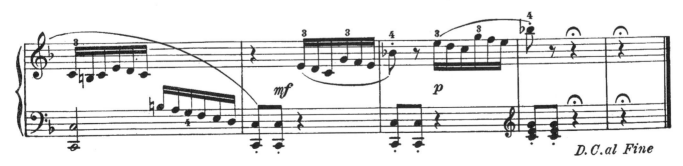

D.C. al Fine

MUZIO CLEMENTI
Sonatina in D Major

(Op. 36, No. 6)

Allegro con spirito

5.

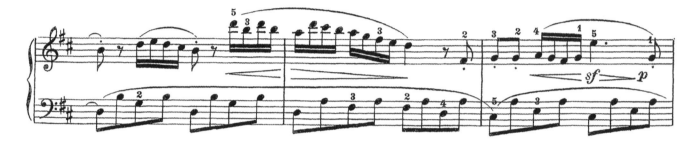

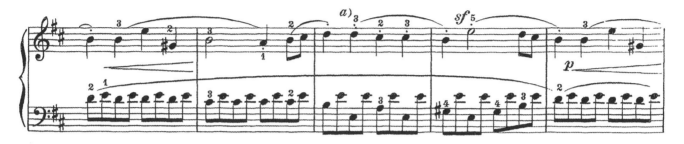

a) Il *portamento* (mezzo legato) su queste quattro note deve essere fatto con espressione: l'allievo deve ottenere un suono dolce ma pieno, senza veruna asprezza, altrimenti la bella frase melodica non avrà più una logica continuità.

a) Le *portamento* sur ces quatre notes doit être fait avec expression: l'élève doit obtenir un son doux mais plein, sans aucune aspérité, autrement la belle phrase mélodique n'aurait plus une continuité logique.

b) Si faccia attenzione a questo *piano* improviso.

b) Faites attention à ce *piano* subit.

a) El *portamento* (semiligado) sobre estas cuatro notas debe ser hecho con expresión El alumno debe obtener un sonido dulce pero lleno, sin ninguna aspereza, pues de otro modo la bella frase melódica perdería su lógica continuidad.

a) The *portamento* (half tied) on these four notes must be done with expression: the pupil must obtain a sweet but full sound, without the slightest harshness, otherwise the beautiful melodic phrase will no longer have a logic continuity.

b) Préstese atención a este *piano* repentino.

b) Put attention to this unexpected *piano*.

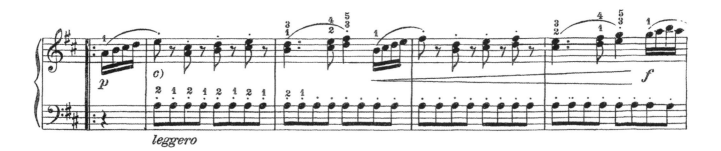

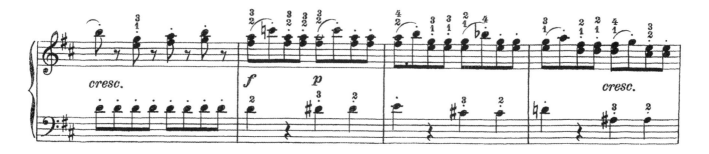

C) Il pollice e l'indice debbono essere situati sulla stessa linea, sopra il *La*. La mano, all'infuori della breve oscillazione dall'alto al basso, non deve avere il minimo movimento laterale.

C) Le pouce et l'index doivent être placés à la même hauteur, au-dessus du *La*. La main, en dehors de la petite oscillation du haut en bas, ne doit pas faire le moindre mouvement latéral.

C) El pulgar y el índice deben estar situados en la misma línea sobre el *La*. Fuera de la breve oscilación de arriba hacia abajo, la mano no debe tener el más mínimo movimiento lateral.

C) The thumb and the fore-finger must be placed on the same line, over the *A*. The hand, except for the brief oscillation from the upper to the lower, must not have the slightest lateral movement.

28

(*d*) Vedi la nota (*b*) a pag. 44.

(*d*) Voyez la note (*b*) à page 44.

d) Véase la nota (*b*) a pag. 44.

d) See note (*b*) page 44.

RONDÒ

Allegretto spiritoso

bene articolato

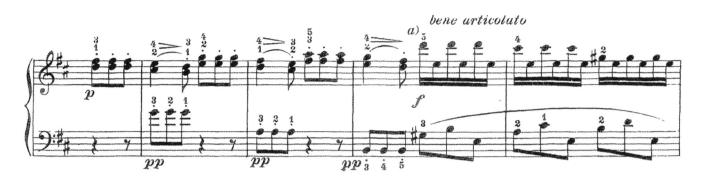

a) Si accenti la parte acuta come se fosse scritta così:

a) Accentuez la partie aiguë comme si elle était écrite ainsi:

a) Acentúese la parte aguda como si estuviera escrita así:

a) Accent the acute part as if written so:

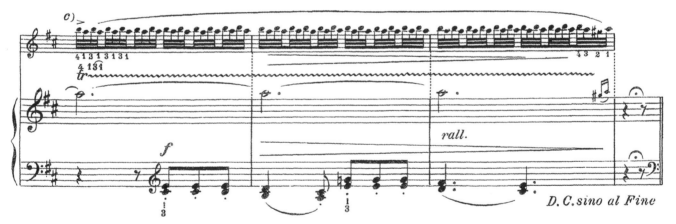

D.C. sino al Fine

b) Si dia molto risalto alla diversità di *colore* e di *carattere* fra questo periodo, quello precedente e quello che segue.

b) *Donnez beaucoup de relief à la différence de* nuance *et de caractère entre cette phrase, celle qui précède et celle qui suit.*

c) Il trillo deve cominciare ben forte: il rallentando e il diminuendo sieno molto sensibili. Le ultime quattro note si eseguiscano lente e pianissimo.

c) *Le trille doit commencer très fort: le rallentando et le diminuendo doivent être très sensibles. Les dernières quatre notes doivent être exécutées avec lenteur et très piano.*

b) *Destáquese bien la diversidad de* color *y de* carácter *entre este período, el precedente y el que sigue.*

b) Put in evidence the difference of colour and character between this period, the preceding and the following.

c) *El trino debe principiar muy fuerte; el rallentando y el diminuendo deben ser muy sensibles. Las últimas cuatro notas: deben ejecutarse con lentitud y muy piano.*

c) The trill must commence well accented: the *rallentando* and the *diminuendo* must be very sensible. The last four notes must be executed slowly and very softly.

MUZIO CLEMENTI
Sonatina in D Major

(Op. 37, No. 2)

6.

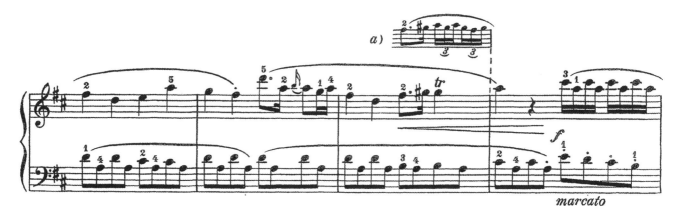

a) Oppure più facile:

a) Ou bien, plus facile:

b) Vedi osservazione *c)* a pag. 45.
b) Voyez remarque *c)* à page 45.

a) O bien, más fácil:

a) Or more easy:

b) Véase observación *c) pag.* 45.
b) See remark *c)* at page 45.

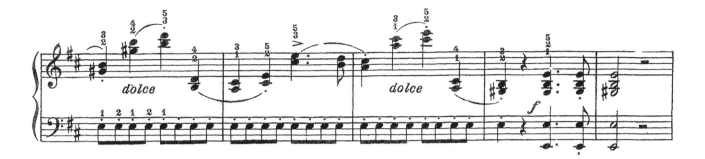

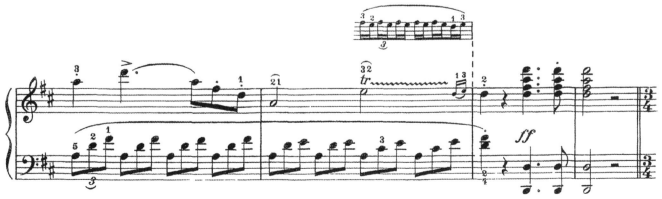

MINUETTO

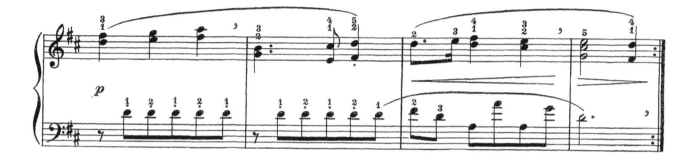

a) Vedi la nota e) a pag. 3.
a) *Voyez la note* e) *à page 3.*

b) Rileggi l'osservazione c) a pag. 45.
b) *Relisez la remarque* c) *à page 45.*

c) Circa il modo di legare queste doppie note rileggi l'osservazione c) pag. 39.
c) *Sur la façon de lier ces doubles notes, relisez la remarque c) a page 39.*

a) *Véase la nota* e) *pag. 3.*
a) See note e) at page 3.

b) *Véase la observación* c) *pag. 45.*
b) Re-read remark c) at page 45.

c) *Sobre el modo de ligar estas dobles notas, véase la observación c) pag. 39.*
c) In regard to the mode of tying these double notes re-read the remark c) at page 39.

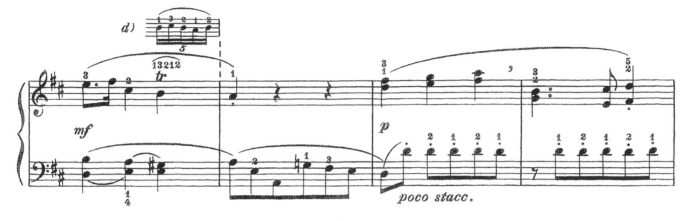

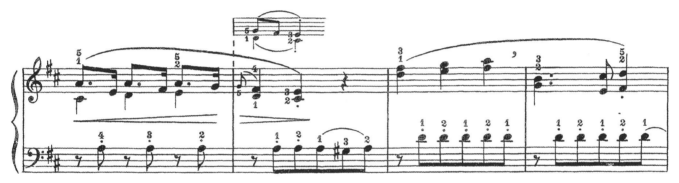

a) Gli allievi che posseggono già un tecnicismo adeguato, preferiscano la seguente diteggiatura:

d) Les élèves qui possèdent déjà une technique suffisamment développée devront préférer le doigté suivant:

d) Los alumnos que poseen ya una técnica adecuada deben adoptar la siguiente digitación:

d) For the pupils who already possess an adequate technique the following fingering is to be preferred:

TRIO

D.C. Minuetto senza replica

e) Le note del primo accordo che possono legarsi perfettamente al secondo sono fa do ; quindi, l'esecuzione è la seguente:

e) Les notes du premier accord qui peuvent se lier parfaitement au second sont fa do ; par conséquent l'exécution sera la suivante

f) Per meglio legare si tenga appoggiato il pollice.

f) Pour mieux lier tenir le pouce appuyé.

e) Las notas del primer acorde que pueden ligarse perfectamente al segundo son fa do. Por tanto la ejecución es la siguiente:

e) The notes of the first chord which can be tied perfectly with those of the second are f c ; therefore the execution is the following:

f) Para ligar mejor manténgase apoyado el pulgar.

f) To tie better, hold down the thumb.

ANTON DIABELLI (1781-1858)

Sonatina in G Major

(Op. 151, No. 1)

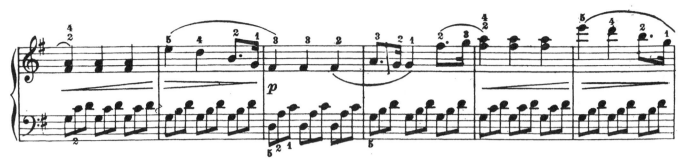

SCHERZO
Allegro

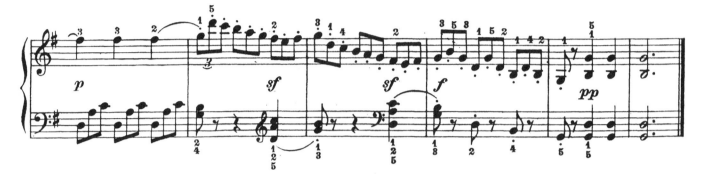

RONDO

Allegretto

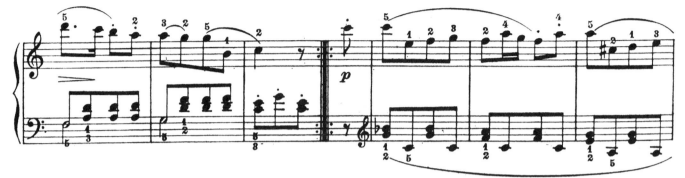

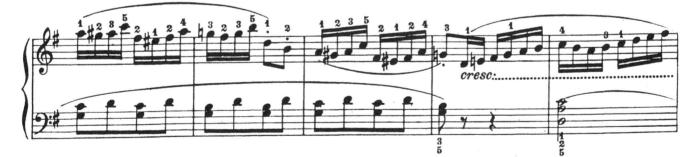

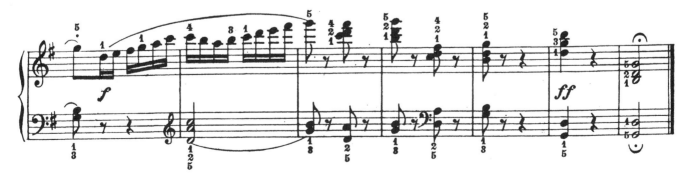

ANTON DIABELLI

Sonatina in C Major

(Op. 151, No. 4)

8.

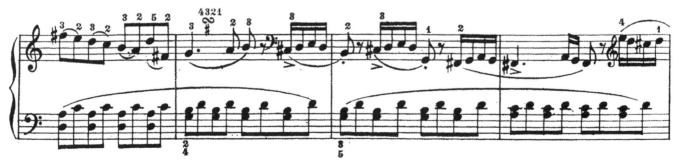

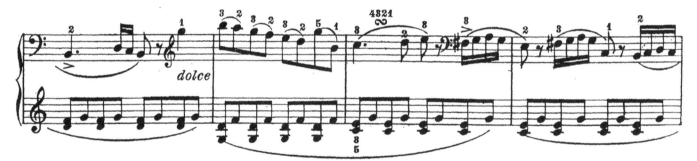

Largo maestoso

RONDO

Allegro, ma non troppo

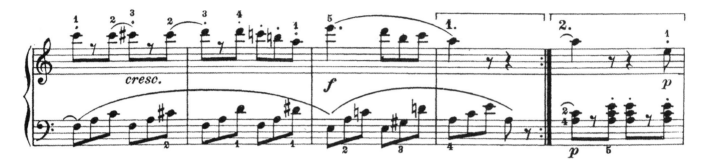

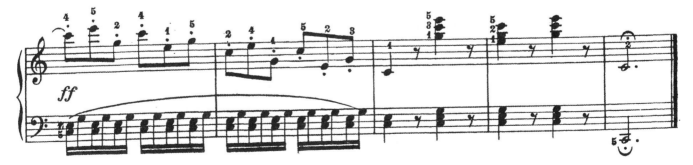

ANTON DIABELLI
Sonatina in D Major

(Op. 168, No. 5)

Tempo di Marcia

9.

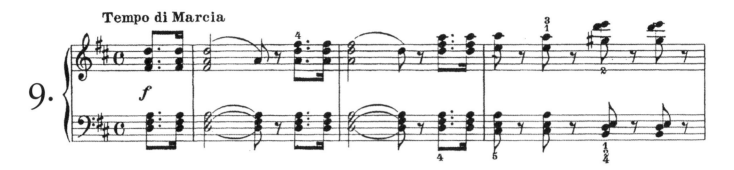

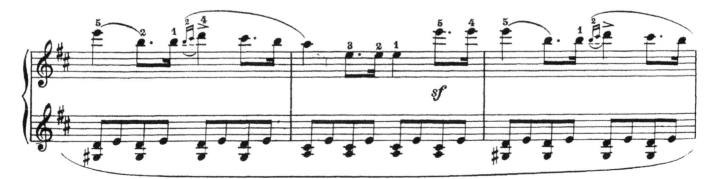

cresc. poco a poco..........................

...... ff

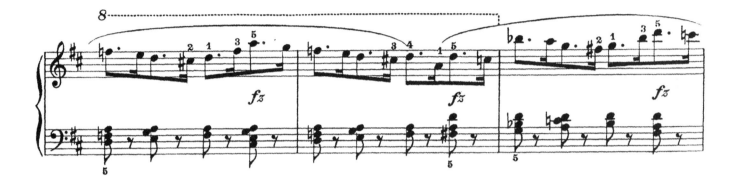

MARCIA FUNEBRE

Andante maestoso

RONDO MILITARE

Allegro

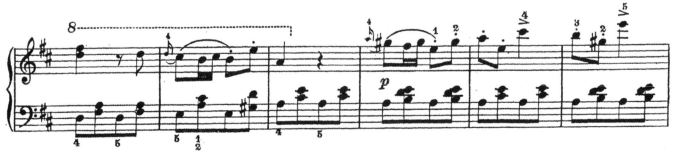

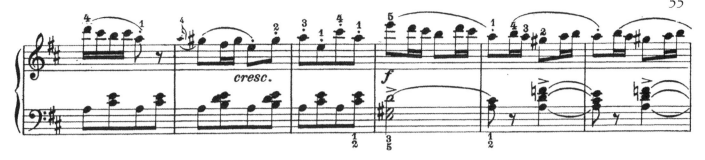

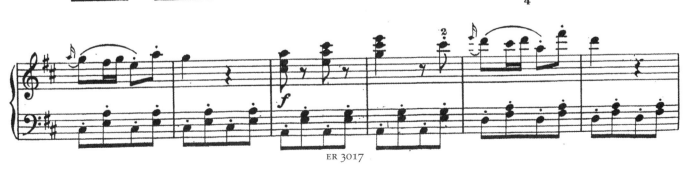

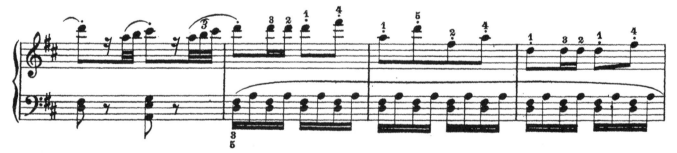

JAN LADISLAW DUSSEK (1760-1812)

Sonatina in G Major

(Op. 20, No. 1)

10.

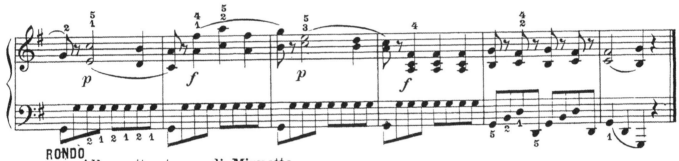

RONDÒ
Allegretto, tempo di Minuetto

MINORE

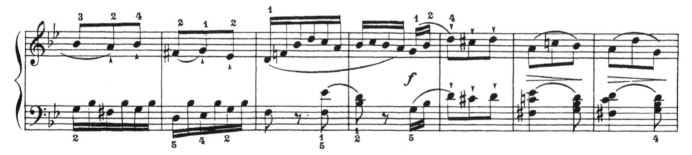

MAGGIORE

FRIEDRICH KUHLAU (1786-1832)

Sonatina in C Major

(Op. 20, No. 1)

11.

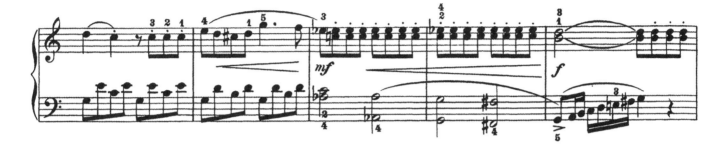

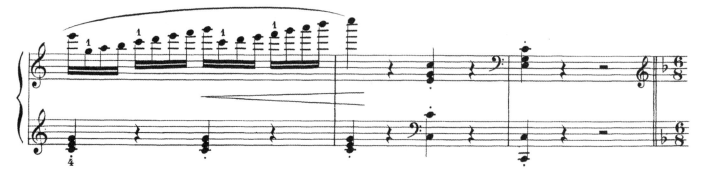

Andante

RONDÒ
Allegro

legato

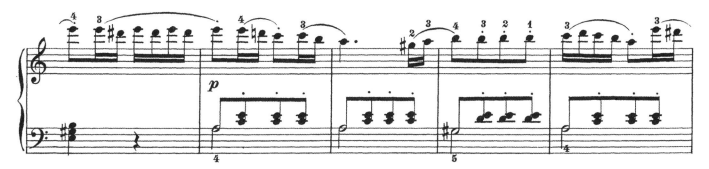

FRIEDRICH KUHLAU
Sonatina in C Major

(Op. 55, No. 1)

12.

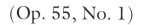

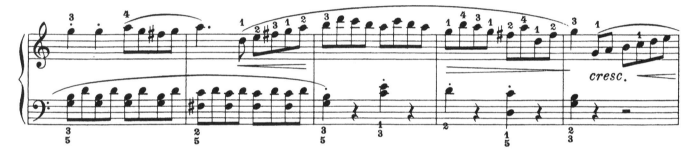
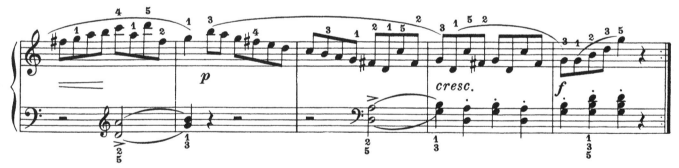

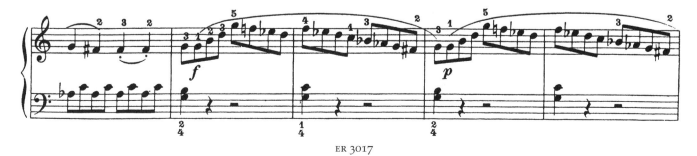

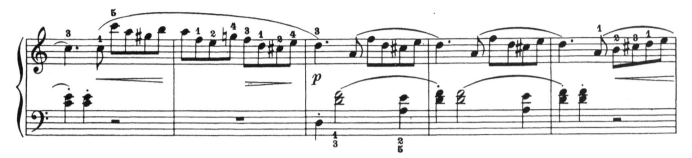

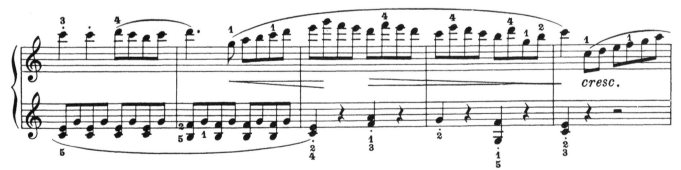

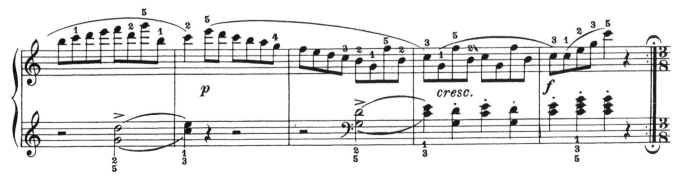

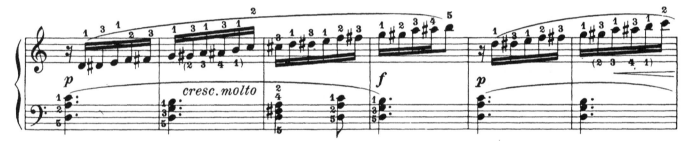

FRIEDRICH KUHLAU
Sonatina in G Major

(Op. 55, No. 2)

13.

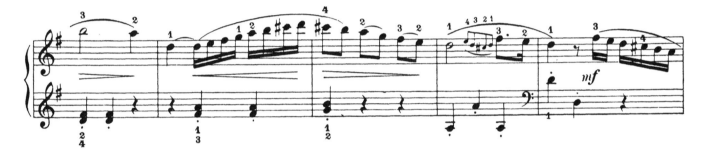

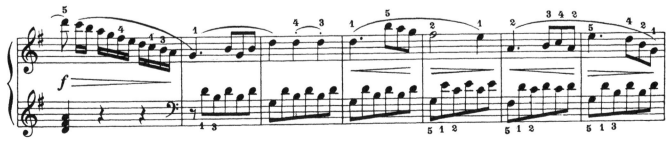

Cantabile

Allegro

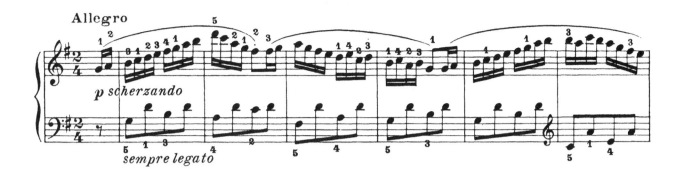

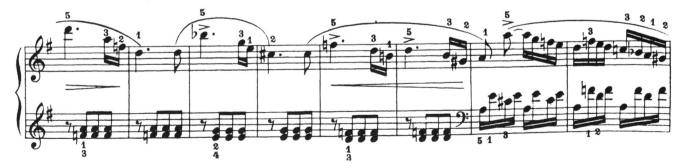

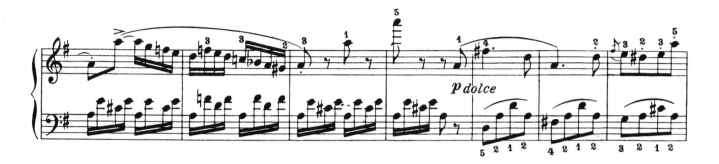

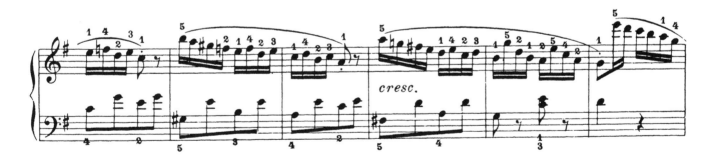

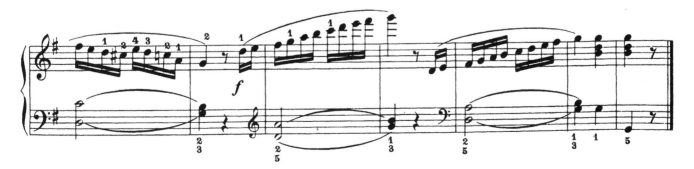

WOLFGANG AMADEUS MOZART (1756-1791)
Sonatina in F Major

(K. 439b)

Menuetto

[**Allegretto** ♩= 144]

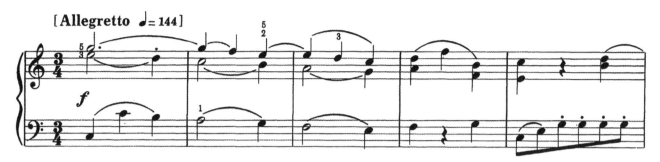

TRIO

Menuetto
da capo

Polonaise

[♩ = 96]